you've made it

EMBRACE the voyage into our fifth stage:

Welcome to a realm where words are not just symbols but alchemical elements designed to transmute your very existence. What you're about to delve into isn't just prose; it's an orchestrated cosmos folded into the fibers of the mundane. Each phrase you encounter is a pivot—imbued with purpose, meant to touch the ineffable while simultaneously shaping your palpable reality.

"**To awaken is not merely to observe reality; it's an existential plunge into the depths of our being, a baptism by life's fires that heralds authentic metamorphosis.**"

Are you prepared to unfold your next chapter, an existential waltz guided by the compass of intuitive wisdom?

Table of Contents

NAMASTE
it's time to wake up

Let's begin this enlightening journey with a POD meditation to help us set a purposeful intention for our minds, bodies, and spirits.

**This is your "Go To" Breathwork POD Meditation
throughout this lesson - revisit this page after each lesson.
(PAUSE OBSERVE DISCERN)**

Find Your Breath, Find Your Center
Begin by settling into a position that encourages both relaxation and alignment. Let your body be fully supported as you close your eyes and shift your focus inward.
Inhale through your nose, deep enough to feel your abdomen rise, filling you with life-giving air. Then, slowly exhale through your lips, releasing any lingering tension or preoccupations. How does that feel?
With each breath, anchor yourself in the immediate now, allowing the present to be your sanctuary.
Next, gently steer your attention to your heart's center. Visualize a soft, luminous light glowing from within, casting a warm embrace around your entire self. As you continue breathing, can you feel its radiance intensifying, infused with love, courage, and self-belief?
As you breathe out, allow this exercise to become a mental sweep, clearing away distractions or anxieties and making room for focus and wisdom. What thoughts or concerns are you willing to release?
Pause here to appreciate your inherent potential. In the rhythm of your breath, reconnect with your unique qualities and strengths. Can you sense an alignment, a symbiosis, between your talents and confidence? Believe in your capability to make a meaningful impact on both your life and the lives of those you touch.
When you sense it's time, gradually open your eyes, but hold onto this enriched state of mind. Your breath isn't just a biological necessity; it's your gateway to self-exploration and metamorphosis.
As you step back into the world, know that this mindful breathing practice is always available, a wellspring of inner clarity and balance. How might you carry this practice into the rest of your day?
So, as you transition back into your surroundings, take these moments of inner peace with you. Whenever life gets overwhelming, remember that your breath is always there: a faithful companion in your journey of self-discovery.

INSTRUCTIONS
for awaken exercises

Starting your day with a connection to your inner spirit is essential, and I'm here to help you achieve that. Our exercises will begin between 4-6 a.m., during the peaceful and tranquil morning hours. These hours are vital as they allow us to be present in the moment and listen to our inner guidance, free of distractions and noise. Let's tune in and silence our thoughts to hear what our source energy tells us.

Let's start by going through each section's journal prompts and then move on to practicing the Awaken breathwork meditation. This meditation is a way to enhance our grace, divinity, and mindfulness. Let's consider it a ritual.

Consider creating a peaceful space in nature for your Awaken exercise! You could opt for your patio, backyard, or even your room with an open window. The key is selecting a location that allows you to awaken purposefully.

To start your practice, stand up and take off your shoes. Connect with the Earth or floor by noticing the cool tile, warm rug, solid concrete, or soft grass under your feet.

Before you start your Awaken meditation, please get comfortable and fully awake for a few minutes. When you feel prepared, you may begin the meditation.

LESSON ONE

Emotional Imagery:
Feel That it's REAL

Objective:

To explore the power of emotional imagery and turn our visions into reality.

A Note of Love:
Reawakening Your Inner Child's Imagination

When was the last time you spent time with your inner child?

Take a pause. Let's connect with that eternally young, vulnerable, and curious facet of you—the inner child. What are they whispering to you today? Could it be a yearning for spontaneity, a call for audacious exploration, or a nudge toward joyful liberation?

As we journey through the years, it's easy to let the wonders of imagination fade into the background. But what if we make it a priority instead? After all, the power to journey through imagined lands and untangle complex realities is a gift that begs to be nurtured and celebrated. How are you nourishing your imagination today?

Your imagination isn't just a whimsical escape; it's a therapeutic powerhouse. Visualization, after all, is a core component of how many of us meditate and manifest. Can you feel how it is deeply woven into your emotional tapestry, forming a unique access point to empathy and creativity?

Imagination is your bridge from the abstract universe of your mind to the tactile world around you. Be it the vivid hues of a sunflower or the surreal whimsy of a red and orange striped elephant donning a top hat—what unrealities are you willing to make real today?

The arena of your mind is fertile ground. Whether you're cultivating sunflowers or striped elephants, remember that your imagination is a realm where anything is possible. So, what are you going to bring to life next?

A Note of Love:
Reawakening Your Inner Child's Imagination

Have you ever paused to dwell on the palpable texture of excitement? It might manifest as a flutter in your stomach, reminiscent of rollercoasters, pulsing crowds, or breathtaking landscapes.

How often do we invoke this emotional cinema when we engage with art forms like music and movies? A horror film might stir a primal fear despite being securely tucked in bed. Contrastingly, a catchy pop tune might turn your kitchen into a dance floor.

So, what's the secret sauce here?

Your imagination doesn't just create; it feels, making your experiences phenomenally real. It is a catalyst for emotional excavation and self-discovery. Can you think of the last time you tapped into this unrealized source of therapeutic creativity?

Now, let's pivot. Close your eyes for a moment and retreat to a place of peace that you've experienced or yearned for. Maybe it's a sunlit beach, the reassuring laughter of people you love, or the solitary joy of a book that speaks your soul. As you visualize, can you also hear it? The rhythmic pounding of waves, the harmonious laughter, or the music that touches your core?

Stay there. Let yourself absorb the saltiness of the ocean air, the warmth of meaningful connection, or the relaxation flowing through your muscles during a massage. Isn't it remarkable how you can summon such tranquility?

Ever ponder what 'peace' really feels like to you? Could it be a sigh of relief, the absence of fear, or perhaps a steady, comforting heartbeat?

Journal Prompts

Answer each prompt with at least 2-3 paragraphs. Give yourself time and space to ask these questions, explore ideas, and use your imagination to answer.

When was the last time you spent quality time with your inner child? What activities can you do to reconnect with their sense of play, adventure, and curiosity?

_____
_____
_____
_____
_____
_____
_____
_____
_____
_____
_____
_____
_____
_____
_____
_____
_____
_____
_____
_____
_____
_____
_____
_____
_____
_____

How does your imagination impact your emotional experiences? Take a moment to reflect on a memory or image that evokes a specific emotion and explore the sensations it brings.

_____
_____
_____
_____
_____
_____
_____
_____
_____
_____
_____
_____
_____
_____
_____

What sentiment is currently taking hold of me? How is this particular emotion sparking the liveliness of my inner child?

_____
_____
_____
_____
_____
_____
_____
_____
_____
_____
_____
_____
_____

In what ways do you use your imagination as a therapeutic tool? How can you incorporate visualization and emotional connection to enhance your meditations and manifestations?

_____
_____
_____
_____
_____
_____
_____
_____
_____
_____
_____
_____
_____
_____
_____
_____
_____
_____

Take a mental journey to a peaceful place or memory. Close your eyes and fully immerse yourself in the experience. What sights, sounds, and sensations do you encounter? How does this moment of peace make you feel?

_____
_____
_____
_____
_____

Reflect on the beauty of sound and its ability to bring tranquility. Visualize the sounds of crashing waves, laughter, or your favorite melody filling your ears. How can you embrace the calming power of sound in your daily life?

_____
_____
_____
_____
_____

Exercise

Begin your AWAKEN exercise between 4-6 a.m.

Find your Awakening space.

Start standing, and ground your bare feet into the Earth or floor beneath you.

When you're ready, practice the Awaken Breathwork Meditation.

LESSON TWO

The Power of Visionary Manifestations:
Energy Manipulation

Objective:

To understand the power of visionary manifestations and manipulate your energy to align with your intentions.

A Note of Love:
Awaken Your Inner Visionary

Awaken is not merely a term but an imperative—a call to inner rebellion against the mundane sediments of existence. It embodies more than wellness; it is a Radical Embrace, a tango with the universe within, where self-expression becomes an act of mindfulness, meditation a political rebellion, and revitalization the nourishment of the soul's perpetual becoming.

Let's dispense with the pedestrian idea that visionaries only come in the guise of industrial magnates or cinematic magicians. A visionary dares to tear through the commonplace fabric to glimpse the ineffable patterns beyond. It's not about inspiration; it's about existential alchemy.

My narrative—stitched with the golden thread of LifePath 11, the chaotic dance of a Heyoka Empath, and the celestial mechanics of a Manifesting Generator—is a single testament in the sacred text of *Being*. Challenges and triumphs are not episodes but stanzas in an eternal poem.

The retreats to Unknown Destinations I offer are neither escapes nor vacations; they're pilgrimages into the soul's labyrinth. You're not a mere participant but a co-conspirator in crafting a bespoke tapestry of transformational modalities. In this intimate crucible, we will stir the pot of your inner wisdom, crystallize insights from the brine of your experience, and unleash the torrent of your creative potential—your brand of cosmic sorcery.

In this sanctum, the alchemy of visionary manifestation isn't a mere outcome; it's the ink with which we rewrite the script of your existence. Each new perspective is a fresh verse in your life's sonnet, each growth spurt a new brushstroke on your existential canvas, and each moment of self-discovery a cosmic note in your lifelong symphony.

A Note of Love:
Awaken Your Inner Visionary

Are You Not More Than a Cosmic Accident?

You find yourself standing on the precipice of potential, the edge of existential inquiry. But before you dive into the celestial waters, dare to carve a sanctuary within your psyche. This is the hallowed ground upon which your connection to the ineffable—be it God, angels, or the raw pulsations of the universe—will be forged. Call it the Alchemist's workshop of the soul, where leaden thoughts transmute into golden wisdom.

Cryptic Dispatches from the Beyond

The world is rife with signs—encrypted messages longing to be deciphered. Do you recognize them? These are not mere coincidences but intimate correspondences from your higher self or source energy. Disconnect from the clamor of existential chaos and listen. To do this, one must adopt a Wittgensteinian lens, understanding that the boundaries of your world are set not merely by language but by attentiveness to the signposts of life itself.

The Will to Elevate

Personal elevation is not a frivolous want but a Nietzschean imperative—a Will to Power of the spirit. To vibrate higher is to shed the cumbersome weight of your earthly limitations. Immerse yourself in atmospheres and energies that are conducive to this divine rebellion. Surround yourself with beings, locations, and endeavors that are inspiring and almost electrifying in their transformative charge.

The Riddle of Being and Becoming

So, what then? Is the journey complete? Of course not. The paradox of existence is that the moment you claim to "Be," you inevitably become a relic of your becoming. As Ram Dass would counsel, focus on the "here and now," the eternal present where being and becoming dance in cosmic harmony.

"In the labyrinth of existence, we are all both seeker and oracle, question and answer fused in cosmic dialogue. May you find not mere paths but dimensions, where every turn is a revelation and every pause a poem unto itself."

Journal Prompts

Answer each prompt with at least 2-3 paragraphs. Give yourself time and space to ask these questions, explore ideas, and use your imagination to answer.

Reflect on your inner journey and the growth you've experienced through the practice of EMBRACE. How have intentional self-expression, mindfulness, and meditation influenced your path as a visionary?

Who are the visionaries you look up to, and what specific qualities or characteristics do they possess that inspire you? How can you incorporate some of these qualities into your own life to awaken your inner visionary?

_____
_____
_____
_____
_____
_____
_____
_____
_____
_____
_____
_____
_____
_____
_____
_____

Explore the challenges and achievements that have shaped your unique life journey. How have these experiences contributed to your ability to embrace visionary manifestations and navigate life's blessings and obstacles?

_____
_____
_____
_____
_____
_____
_____
_____
_____
_____
_____
_____

Take a moment to connect with your intuition and emotional imagery. How does your intuitive connection to energy influence your perspectives and decision-making as you embark on your sacred journey of self-discovery?

_____

_____

_____

_____

_____

_____

_____

_____

_____

_____

_____

_____

_____

_____

_____

Envision yourself on a transformative 1:1 wellness retreat to an Unknown Destination. Describe how this journey would empower you to awaken your inner visionary.

_____

_____

_____

_____

_____

_____

_____

_____

_____

_____

_____

Exercise

Begin your exercise between 4-6 a.m.

Find your Awakening space.

Start in a standing position, and ground your bare feet into the Earth or floor beneath you.

When you're ready, practice the Awaken Breathwork Meditation.

A Note of Love:
What is Your Purpose?

Soul Seat: Imagine your hand gently resting upon your Tan Tien, that secret cauldron of vitality near your navel. Elevate your other hand to your Soul Seat—the sanctuary perched between the heart's labyrinth and the voice's altar. Picture an ethereal filament tethering these two realms, pulsating with the essence of your 'why,' the primordial yearning sculpting your existential architecture.

Individuation Nexus: The term "individuation" whispers its legacy from Latin—a tongue ancient as the concept itself. "Individuus," a sentinel guarding the notion of the "indivisible." As you traverse the eldritch corridors of soul retrieval, seize the paradox of Becoming Nobody. In this existential vacuum, your boundless potential shall echo back to you, revealing fragments of your reclaimed soul.

The Hara Continuum is not just a line but a cosmic string, a trinity of nodal points linking you to the cosmic loom of existence. It's your umbilical cord to the source, your North Star guiding you to purpose, and your anchor tethering you to Earthly reality. It's the axis upon which your universe spins.

Misalignment in your Hara Continuum manifests as existential dissonance. A thirst for an unknown 'more,' a descent into the abyss of purposelessness, the haunting specter of aloneness. Yet, alignment metamorphoses this disarray into rooted certitude. You no longer hunger for external validation; you sup on existential authenticity.

Your Soul Seat—your existential epicenter—radiates increasingly vivid luminosity as you forge connections skyward through your Individuation Nexus and earthward through your Tan Tien.

In the cosmic ballet, purpose isn't found—it's woven. Align your inner stars, and 'what you seek' becomes 'what you are.'

Journal Prompts

Answer each prompt with at least 2-3 paragraphs. Give yourself time and space to ask these questions, explore ideas, and use your imagination to answer.

Take a few deep breaths and place your hand on your Tan Tien, then slowly raise the other hand to your Soul Seat. Close your eyes and visualize the connection between these points. What does this connection represent to you? How does it relate to your aspirations and inner perception?

_____
_____
_____
_____
_____
_____
_____
_____
_____
_____
_____
_____
_____
_____
_____
_____
_____
_____
_____
_____
_____
_____
_____

Reflect on the concept of "individuation" and what it means to you. How have external factors influenced your sense of self in the past? How can embracing Becoming Nobody help you reclaim your authentic essence and tap into your untapped potential?

_____

_____

_____

_____

_____

_____

_____

_____

_____

_____

_____

_____

_____

_____

_____

_____

Consider the Hara Line and its significance in connecting you to your source energy, purpose, and the Earth and Heavens. How do you feel grounded and centered when aligned with your Hara Line? How does this alignment affect your overall sense of well-being and inner strength?

_____

_____

_____

_____

_____

_____

_____

_____

_____

_____

_____

Think about a time when your Hara Line felt out of alignment. How did it manifest in your life? What were the challenges you faced during that period? How did you work towards realigning with your purpose and source power?

_____

_____

_____

_____

_____

_____

Imagine your purpose and Soul Seat growing brighter as you strengthen your connection with Mother Earth. What steps can you take to nurture this alignment and fully embrace your soul's purpose? How will this transformation impact other aspects of your life, relationships, and personal growth journey?

_____

_____

_____

_____

_____

_____

Exercise

Begin your exercise between 4-6 a.m.

Find your Awakening space.

Start in a standing position, and ground your bare feet into the Earth
or floor beneath you.

When you're ready, practice the Awaken Breathwork Meditation.

LESSON FOUR

Becoming Nobody

Objective:

To surrender our egos to free ourselves from
the regrets, demands, and pressure of the
past and future to "be here now."

A Note of Love:
What is Your Purpose?

In the vast cosmic theater, the ultimate role isn't to star as 'Somebody.' It's to artfully vanish into 'Nobody,' where purpose isn't scripted but arises from the ineffable dialogue between one's essence and the universe.

The Weltanschauung peddled by society often dictates: 'Ascend the pedestal of fame to cast a shadow.' Such a myopic lens, isn't it? True gravitas, that seismic resonance, emanates not from the gallery's applause but from the quiet alchemy of inner harmony.

In the theater of existence, consider the radical act of Becoming Nobody. Here, unshackled by the gargantuan ego and societal mirages, your singular essence transcends into a universal chorus. The quest shifts—from the banal vanity of 'becoming somebody' to the sublime serenity of an existential metamorphosis, one that embraces a pulsating oneness with the cosmic lattice.

When you cease to ornament your existence with the detritus of 'shoulds' and 'could haves,' the here and now crystallizes into a sanctuary. It's a cathedral where the hymns are your ever-evolving breaths, thoughts, and very being. Serving, passion, existence—these are the liturgies that transmute 'enough' into plenitude.

Much like Ram Dass's musings on mortality—the untying of life's 'tight shoe' as neither tragedy nor epilogue but a poignant stanza in the ballad of being. Death isn't a realm for a Death Doula but a poetic verse for an Ascension Shaman like me.

Final thought? Pivot with intent. EMBRACE to transcend. Transmute grief into grace—a celestial choreography where every step is purpose incarnate.

"Death, not an end, but a threshold—
A door to dimensions yet unseen.
In becoming nobody, we inherit the cosmos,
Life's greatest, yet most elusive scene." Ram Dass

The Power of The POD:
Unlocking Inner Wisdom through Pause Observation and Discernment

The POD—is more than an acronym; it's a pilgrimage to 'Non-being,' an odyssey beyond the ego.

PAUSE: It's not mere stillness; it's a resolute cessation from the world's ceaseless chatter, a mutiny against distraction. In this sacred void, you unhinge the masks, unraveling the Gordian knots of outward identity. The quietude is not an absence but a potent space—infused with potentialities.

OBSERVE: Witness, don't just see. This stage isn't passive watching; it actively decouples from societal narratives and self-constructed fiction. It's a lucid awareness, devoid of judgment, where you dissect your programmed ideologies, your conceptual wardrobe. What remains is not the fabricated 'you' but a distilled essence—a noumenal self beyond societal contours.

DISCERNMENT: This is your existential compass, your soul's barometer. It transcends mere choice; it's an alignment—a magnetic pull toward what genuinely resonates with your innermost frequencies. It dissolves the validation quest, defying societal yardsticks of what counts as a 'life well-lived.'

In traversing the POD pathway, you're not just reaching a destination but dissolving into the journey itself. You're shedding the egoic shell, tearing down the facades of societal validation, and soaring into an existence not confined by nouns or adjectives. You're not becoming a better version of yourself; you're becoming 'Nobody,' which paradoxically makes you a universal 'Somebody.'

That is the crux—through POD, you unearth existential freedom, liberating you from identities to unite with your most unadulterated Self. Here, you touch the intangible—your indefinable purpose, and from this space, you cease to be a mere role and become a cosmic force.

"In the stillness of pause, the wisdom of observation meets the clarity of discernment, illuminating the path to authentic purpose."

Journal Prompts

Answer each prompt with at least 2-3 paragraphs. Give yourself time and space to ask these questions, explore ideas, and use your imagination to answer.

Pause and Reflect: Take a moment of quietude each day to cultivate space for self-contemplation. How does this practice of the POD help you disengage from external distractions and connect with your authentic self?

_____

_____

_____

_____

_____

_____

_____

_____

_____

_____

_____

_____

_____

_____

_____

_____

_____

_____

_____

_____

_____

_____

_____

_____

_____

_____

The Power of Observation: Practice observing your thoughts, feelings, and habits without judgment or criticism. What insights have you gained from this habit of objective observation? How has it impacted your self-concept and sense of purpose?

_____

_____

_____

_____

_____

_____

_____

_____

_____

_____

_____

_____

_____

_____

_____

Embracing Discernment: Listen to the call of your inner sanctuary, intuitive sense, and higher wisdom when making choices. How has discernment guided you to make decisions that resonate with your true self? How does it help you align with your core beliefs and lead a meaningful life?

_____

_____

_____

_____

_____

_____

_____

_____

_____

_____

_____

Unveiling Your Authentic Self: Reflect on the transformative journey of "becoming nobody." How has learning about "The POD" modality allowed you to shed layers of external self-definition and societal pressures? How does living from a place of inner harmony enable you to recognize and embrace your authentic self fully?

_____
_____
_____
_____
_____
_____
_____
_____
_____
_____
_____
_____
_____
_____
_____
_____
_____

Exercise

Begin your exercise between 4-6 a.m.

Find your Awakening space.

Start in a standing position, and ground your bare feet into the Earth
or floor beneath you.

When you're ready, practice the Awaken Breathwork Meditation.

LESSON FIVE

Impermanence:
Life's Great Wake–Up Call

Objective:

To embrace the beauty of impermanence
and begin to live our lives to the fullest.

A Note of Love:
Nothing Is Permanent
(and that's okay)

Embracing Impermanence

In the theater of fleeting time,
Where Change pens each unfolding rhyme,
We dance between the here and gone
A twilight kiss, a breaking dawn.

Why dread the falling of the leaf,
When autumn paints, its bold relief?
Or mourn the melting of the snow,
When spring's first buds have room to grow?

Each ending whispers to us, "See,
You're but a fleeting melody."
In impermanence, we find
The sacred hymns of humankind.

So let us meet each shifting tide,
No longer seeking place to hide.
Embrace the Now—our truest home—
And find in Change, we're never alone.

In our obsessive quest for permanence, we forge iron-clad contracts and calcify routines as though we could stave off the inevitable tides of Change—the primordial alchemy of existence. These artifices of control are but sandcastles before the oceanic flux of life; beautiful, yes, but fated to erode.

We hold our breath in ephemeral euphoria, naive to the hurricane of Change that churns in the distance—until it roars ashore, dismantling our mirages.

Ah, don't mistake me for a cynic. Impermanence is not a tragic footnote but the ink with which life is written. It's the leitmotif of our existence, an invitation to dance in the theater of the Now. Each change we lament is but a death, and each death
a doorway—an ethos deeply etched in the cyclical philosophies of Buddhism.

When you resist Change, you chain yourself to the illusion of continuity. Break free. Acknowledge impermanence as your co-conspirator, not your foe. Instead of fossilizing plans, see them as fluid blueprints for reality yet to be sculpted. You're not losing; you're shedding, metamorphosing, evolving.

Give room to your sorrows, but don't let them build homes in you. Beauty is a passing landscape, as is suffering—a series of transitory brushstrokes on the grand canvas of existence.

And so, wake up to this impermanent symphony and make each cadence, each crescendo, and each silent pause truly yours. Abandon regret; it's a relic of a past self who didn't know better. Embrace the current moment as a radical act of rebellion against impermanence.

To live as if each moment is orchestrated in your favor—that, my friend, is the closest we come to touching eternity.

Journal Prompts

Answer each prompt with at least 2-3 paragraphs. Give yourself time and space to ask these questions, explore ideas, and use your imagination to answer.

Embracing Impermanence: Reflect on the concept of impermanence and its significance in Buddhism. How can embracing the idea that nothing is intended to last forever add value and beauty to your life? How can you cultivate a mindset that welcomes change and views it as an opportunity for growth?

_____
_____
_____
_____
_____
_____
_____
_____
_____
_____
_____
_____
_____
_____
_____
_____
_____
_____
_____
_____
_____
_____
_____

Living in the Present: Consider the quote by Rumi, "Live life as if everything is rigged in your favor." How can adopting this perspective empower you to live fully in the present moment and let go of regrets or fears about the future? How can you find joy and purpose in each moment, despite the inevitable changes that life brings?

_____
_____
_____
_____
_____
_____
_____
_____
_____
_____
_____
_____
_____
_____
_____

Exercise

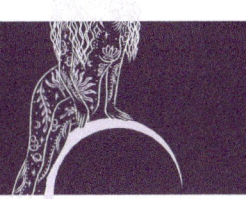

Begin your exercise between 4-6 a.m.

Find your Awakening space.

Start in a standing position, and ground your bare feet into the Earth or floor beneath you.

When you're ready, practice the Awaken Breathwork Meditation.

LESSON SIX

The Path to Enlightenment

Objective:

To embrace the beauty of impermanence
and begin to live our lives to the fullest.

A Note of Love:
Your Path to Enlightenment

Enlightenment—less a destination, more an ever-unfolding tapestry. This path is not linear but fractal, tracing infinite patterns of awareness and consciousness. Your odyssey toward enlightenment is etched with paradoxes, fueled by the sublime and the mundane and elevated by authentic introspection.

Here, HUMILITY manifests not as self-deprecation but as an existential surrender, a yielding to the unfathomable grandeur of existence itself. In the shedding of illusionary veils, we find not absence but our untamed essence.

TRUTH, then, is your North Star in this labyrinthine journey. It doesn't pacify but agitates, urging you towards the unbalanced equilibrium where chaos and order commingle, perpetually inviting wholeness.

In the throes of CONNECTION, we're neither rootless wanderers nor static trees but the ever-expanding mycelium—our lives a complex web of relationships that feed our source power and amplify our existential resonance.

Through the lens of TRUST, the universe ceases to be a foreign expanse and transmutes into an intimate landscape. It is a symphony of synchronicities where each dissonant or harmonious note enriches the existential score.

GRATITUDE emerges not merely as an attitude but as a radical acceptance. It recognizes the intricate ballet of sorrow and joy, agony and ecstasy, as the fabric of our human tapestry.

ASPIRATION, then, is not about reaching an apex but spiraling inward and outward. The gyroscope navigates us through the liminal, eternally sculpting our cosmic self-portrait.

Within this unfathomable journey unfolds COMPASSION—a fierce tenderness that transcends sentimentality. It becomes a subversive act, an anarchic kindness that defies conditional metrics and enfolds us all in its boundless embrace.

So, let us be wayfarers on this enigmatic path.

And for your Morning Theta Meditation, consider:
"In the stillness of my heart, I touch eternity.
Present in the Now, I honor the sepia hues of yesterday.
Present in the Now, I untangle the nebulous threads of tomorrow.
Present in the Now, I become the artisan of my becoming."

Journal Prompts

Answer each prompt with at least 2-3 paragraphs. Give yourself time and space to ask these questions, explore ideas, and use your imagination to answer.

Humility: Have I made my life needlessly complex? If I have, what are the reasons behind it?

_____
_____
_____
_____
_____
_____
_____
_____
_____
_____
_____
_____
_____
_____
_____
_____
_____
_____
_____
_____
_____
_____
_____
_____

Truth: What truth do I need to give careful consideration to?

_____
_____
_____
_____
_____
_____
_____
_____
_____
_____
_____
_____
_____
_____
_____
_____
_____

Connection: What must be shed from the outer layers of my life so that my inner radiance can glow radiantly?

_____
_____
_____
_____
_____
_____
_____
_____
_____
_____
_____
_____
_____

Trust: What should I release or embrace to strengthen my connection with faith?

_____
_____
_____
_____
_____
_____
_____
_____
_____
_____
_____
_____
_____
_____
_____
_____

Gratitude: What am I waiting for? How can I break free from waiting and embrace a more fulfilling life going forward?

_____
_____
_____
_____
_____
_____
_____
_____
_____
_____
_____
_____

Aspiration: How can I inspire the aspiration to embrace all the creation within and around me?

_____
_____
_____
_____
_____
_____
_____
_____
_____
_____
_____
_____
_____
_____
_____
_____
_____
_____
_____

Compassion: How can I incorporate acts of loving-kindness into my daily life?

_____
_____
_____
_____
_____
_____
_____
_____
_____
_____
_____
_____
_____
_____

AWAKEN
CLOSING PRAYER

Dear Universe, Divine Source, and all that is sacred,

As we gather here at the culmination of our Awaken journey, we offer gratitude for the wisdom and insight gained. We acknowledge the divine presence that guided us through these transformative moments.

We thank you for the clarity and self-discovery we've found within the embrace of each breath. We recognize the light within us, reflecting your eternal wisdom and grace.

As we close this chapter, we ask for your continued guidance and blessings on our paths. May the lessons we've learned during our time together continue to illuminate our way forward.

Grant us the strength to carry the mindfulness and self-belief we've cultivated into the world. May we use these gifts to create positive change in our lives and th those we touch.ose we touch.

We release any doubts or fears that hold us back and embrace the courage to step into the next phase of our journey. May we carry the lessons of this Awaken stage with us as we navigate the world's challenges and joys.

In your infinite wisdom, help us to turn the page with grace, knowing that we are forever connected to the wisdom within us and the guidance of the cosmos.

Thank you for this time of self-discovery, growth, and transformation. May we walk this path with open hearts and minds, ready to embrace the new beginnings that await.

With Loving Intentions, My Body, My Mind, My Spirit.

We are now entering the last stage of grief, Eat Healthy, Warriors,

Journeys can take straightforward routes, while others meander through uncertainty. Sometimes, people come together to lend support and lighten the burden. Regardless of the challenges we face on our journeys, there's an opportunity to reach a particular destination—a place where our innermost desires align with our soul's longing—where we find a radiant glow of unconditional love.

Let us acknowledge and honor the paths we've traversed and those that lie ahead as we awaken to the present moment.

With Purposeful Intentions,

MiMi

Please explore a my healing jewelry collection & more self-love adornments. The UNALOME symbolizes the path toward enlightenment, and each piece is designed as a reminder of the inner strength and courage we all possess.
Visit www.StoryOf11.com to discover these meaningful creations.

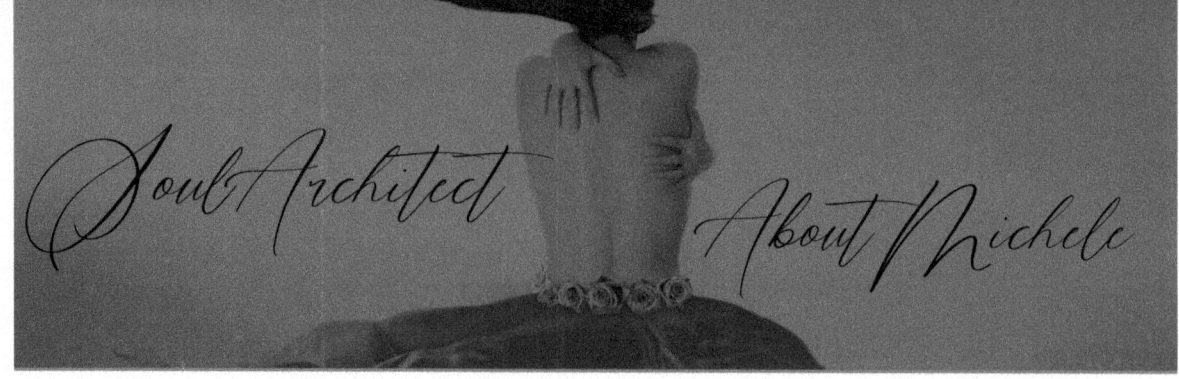

Michele C. Bell's narrative is a profound testament to resilience, the transformative power of embracing life's most profound challenges, and the depth of human compassion. Her journey, which began with the deeply personal and original work "*A Journey of Unconditional Love,*" evolved into the 22-time award-winning story, "*A Son's Gift,*" marking the inception of her distinguished career as an empathetic voice within the realm of grief literature.

With a Ph.D. in Philosophy and Metaphysics, Michele brings a unique blend of intuitive insight and scholarly depth to "*The 7 Stages of Grief* - **EMBRACE**." This work, unlike traditional grief literature, opens a space where healing is interwoven with personal growth and transformation, guided by Michele's own experiences, her profound journey through PTSD, and her scholarly insights. This journey has not only deepened her understanding of grief and resilience but also infused her writing with authenticity and compassion, offering solace and a transformative roadmap to those navigating the intricacies of loss.

Her innovative approach, blending the profound depths of intuitive philosophy with avant-garde grief counseling modalities, pioneers a novel paradigm in grief literature. Michele's work, transcending meticulous writing and exploration, charts a path towards transformative healing. Each stage, encapsulated within the evocative acronym **EMBRACE**, is meticulously crafted to guide the bereaved with dignity, offering nuanced understanding through the labyrinth of loss.

Beyond her literary contributions, Michele's life story—marked by resilience amidst adversity—enriches her professional narrative. From facing challenges such as bullying and domestic abuse to navigating the complexities of being a holistic real estate broker, Michele's experiences underscore her innate desire to support individuals through significant life transitions. The profound loss of her son to Ewings Sarcoma tested her resolve, catalyzing a shift towards mental health advocacy and the development of groundbreaking methodologies like the Soul Design technique and the *7 Stages of Grief* workbooks.

Michele's contributions extend to her active involvement in suicide prevention and domestic abuse programs, where her voice has become a force for change. Her purpose, whether as a holistic real estate broker, end-of-life expert, or mental health advocate, remains consistent—to support, guide, and uplift. As a member and keynote speaker for the **Daughters of Penelope**, Michele shares inspiring messages of healing, humor, and love, emphasizing the necessity of such virtues in today's world.

At 58, Michele C. Bell, The Grief Warrior®, stands as a testament to the enduring power of the human spirit, commanding respect and fostering deep, authentic connections. Her life experiences, granting her the invaluable CAT credentials of **Compassion, Authenticity, and Trust**, continue to inspire those fortunate enough to encounter her work.

Testimonial

I have been blessed to know Michele—a woman of unshakable spirit, dignity, and beauty.

Michele has navigated serious challenges in her early life, creating a beautiful world where she continues to thrive. Raising her children single-handedly and advancing her vocation, she blends rich creativity and imagination with outstanding professional skills.

Michele possesses a powerful intuition, akin to a sixth sense, that has supported many individuals. She has dedicated her spirit and skills to serve others, positively impacting numerous lives. Moreover, her loyalty is unparalleled.

I wholeheartedly endorse my dear friend to advocate, consult, or speak on inspiring topics. Her presence radiates an elegant energy that transforms any gathering.

-JULIAN LAMPERT, CLASSICAL PIANIST

DISCLAIMER

All content within the 7 Stages of Grief Alignment Workbook is original and intended solely to promote mind, body, and spirit well-being. This material does not replace the expertise or advice of a licensed mental health professional. Grief experiences are unique to each individual, and while the workbook provides supportive tools and perspectives, it does not guarantee specific outcomes. If you are experiencing intense or extreme distress, please consult a professional.

By using this course, you acknowledge and accept these terms and conditions. The 7 Stages of Grief certification program, conceived and developed by Dr. Michele Bell, offers an innovative, holistic, and empathy-driven approach to understanding and navigating grief. It is rooted in comprehensive research and deep insight into the human experience of loss and recovery.

Program Overview:
- Embracing Growth in Grief: Recognize the transformative potential within grief.
- The 7 Stages of Grief: Explore the intricate emotional journey of grief, encompassing its multifaceted seven stages.
- Pivoting with Purpose: Equip yourself with practical tools to channel grief's raw energy into purposeful action.
- Understanding the Power of Resistance: Gain insights into the obstacles resistance can pose on the healing journey and learn strategies to address and overcome it.
- Coping Modalities: Discover and apply various coping methods tailored to individual grief journeys or to assist others on this path.
- Certification: As a culmination, the program offers a certification examination to ensure a comprehensive understanding of the 7 Stages of Grief methodology.

Engage with the 7 Stages of Grief, All-In-One Master Compilation program to acquire a compassionate and informed approach to navigating the intricate labyrinth of grief, whether for personal growth or as a professional commitment.

Remember, every voice matters in bringing light to the shadows of grief. By uniting, we can raise awareness and create a world where everyone feels understood and supported during their moments of profound loss. I deeply appreciate your commitment to this cause. Please take a moment to sign the **Loss Awareness Day** petition on **Change.org**, inspired by the heartfelt endeavors of Lisa Marie Presley. Together, we can make a difference.
With heartfelt gratitude and hope,
MiMi + The Grief Warrior®